Thank You Mother Nature

By: Charlotte Caunter

WTL INTERNATIONAL

Copyright © 2018 Charlotte Caunter

All rights reserved. No part of this publication may be reproduced in any form or by any electronic or mechanical means including information storage and material systems, except in the case of brief quotations embodied in critical articles or reviews, without permission in writing from its publisher, WTL International.

Illustrations: Page 3 (flowers) courtesy of belchonock © 123RF.COM; Page 5 © Makhnach_S/Shutterstock.com; Page 13 courtesy of Loopall © 123RF.COM; Page 15 © NEILRAS/Shutterstock.com; Page 17 © Celana/Shutterstock.com; Page 19 © ActiveLines/Shutterstock.com; Page 21 courtesy of kreta37 © 123RF.COM; Page 23 (cracked dirt background) courtesy of Kheng Guan Toh © 123RF.COM; Page 29 (animals) courtesy of macrovector © 123RF.COM; Page 31 © rvika/Shutterstock.com; Page 35 courtesy of rvika © 123RF.COM; Page 37 © dibrova/Shutterstock.com; Page 41 © kikoo/Shutterstock.com; All other images © Aisha Hammah of WTL International's Cutie Fruity Illustrations™.

Library and Archives Canada Cataloguing in Publication

Caunter, Charlotte, 1978-, author
Thank you Mother Nature / Charlotte Caunter.

ISBN 978-1-927865-09-5 (paperback)

1. Nature--Juvenile literature. 2. Natural history--Juvenile literature. I. Title.

QH48.C38 2015   j508   C2015-907221-2

Published by
WTL International
930 North Park Drive
P.O. Box 33049
Brampton, Ontario
L6S 6A7 Canada

www.wtlipublishing.com

ISBN 978-1-927865-09-5

Printed in Canada and the USA

10 9 8 7 6 5 4 3 2 1

Thank you, Mother Nature, for giving us the most striking sun. Every time I see the sun, it reminds me of all of the energy you give to the planet. It also reminds me that no matter where we live on this earth, we all share the same sun.

Thank you, Mother Nature, for giving us the magnificent moon. Every time I see the moon, it reminds me to stay positive because even in darkness there can be light.

Thank you, Mother Nature, for giving us so many sparkling stars. Every time I see the stars, they remind me to make a wish and to dream **BIG**, as dreams really do come true.

Thank you, Mother Nature, for giving us the wonderful wind. Every time I feel the wind, it reminds me to stay cool and enjoy life. The wind gives us energy, makes the trees dance, and even allows us to do things like fly kites.

Thank you, Mother Nature, for giving us fantastic fire. Every time I see fire, it reminds me that it gives us light and keeps us warm. It also reminds me to smile to spread my light to others.

Thank you, Mother Nature, for giving us wonderful water. Every time I see water, it reminds me that it helps give life to plants, animals and people. Water is also magical to our bodies. It can help clean us up when we're dirty and quench our thirst when we're thirsty.

Thank you, Mother Nature, for all of our terrific trees. Every time I see a tree, it reminds me they clean our air. Sometimes I stop what I'm doing and take in a big, refreshing, deep breath to appreciate what they do for us.

Thank you, Mother Nature, for giving us wonderful waterfalls. Every time I see a waterfall, it reminds me that this huge, magical piece of nature only started with one drop of water. I am reminded that in the same way, even one small positive action can become a part of something great and magical.

Thank you, Mother Nature, for giving us regal rainbows. Every time I see a rainbow, it reminds me that something beautiful always happens after a storm.

Thank you, Mother Nature, for giving us robust rocks. Every time I see a rock, it reminds me that many of them hold stories of our past which can help us now. Maybe my story will one day help others too.

Thank you, Mother Nature, for giving us so many beautiful birds. Every time I see a bird, it reminds me to stop and listen to their charming music and to keep my eyes towards the skies.

Thank you, Mother Nature, for giving us lots of buzzing bees. Every time I see a bee, it reminds me that no matter how little you feel, you can help many others. Bees help plants, animals and even people.

Thank you, Mother Nature, for giving us many different types of amazing animals. Every time I see an animal, I am reminded that we share this world with other splendid creatures apart from ourselves. Their dependence on us reminds me to be kind to animals and this reminds me that I must also be kind, gentle and caring to every person I meet.

Thank you, Mother Nature, for giving us the fantastic season of fall. Every fall reminds me to pay attention to all the different colours that are around me. When I see a leaf fall, it reminds me to accept endings so I can make room for wonderful new beginnings.

Thank you, Mother Nature, for giving us the wonderful season of winter. Every winter makes me cuddle up to family to stay warm. Winter reminds me that change can happen very quickly and other times, it requires patience. Even when I have doubt, I can be sure something superb is just around the corner.

Thank you, Mother Nature, for giving us the superb season of spring. Every spring reminds me to appreciate the beauty all around me and to even look at the beauty I possess within me. I am kind, smart, loving, and helpful to others. As I look within, I realize the more I love me just as I am, the more I will help others to love and accept themselves too.

Thank you, Mother Nature, for giving us the sensational season of summer. Every summer, I am reminded to be grateful for everything and everyone around me as I am surrounded by abundance—an abundance of grass, flowers, sunshine fresh air and blue skies.

Thank you, Mother Nature, for giving us a variety of fresh foods. Every time I see the food you provide, I am reminded you help us stay full, healthy and strong. Food gives us energy and can make us feel good.

Thank you, Mother Nature, for giving us so many different types of phenomenal people. Every time I see someone, I know that no matter what we look like, where we live or how much money we have, everyone is special, smart and beautiful. We can all learn from each other.

Thank you, Mother Nature, for all that you do for us! Every time I notice nature around me, it reminds me to respect you and appreciate you for all of your magical powers, your inspirational beauty, your wonderful reminders and your nourishment.

You do so much for us! What can I do to help you?

I know! I will help protect you by taking steps like recycling; turning off the water when I brush my teeth; planting trees; re-using my water bottle instead of buying plastic ones; using reusable bags; walking, biking or carpooling to school; turning off all my electronic devices at night; and by bringing my lunches to school in reusable containers.

One person can make a difference and I want to be that person.

Lots of love and a **BIG** hug,
Me
xoxo

www.ingramcontent.com/pod-product-compliance
Lightning Source LLC
Chambersburg PA
CBHW061400090426
42743CB00002B/78